PIANO • VOCAL • GUITAR

2nd Edition

COUNTRY SONGS
OF Faith, Hope & Love

ISBN 978-1-4950-6325-1

HAL•LEONARD®
CORPORATION
7777 W. BLUEMOUND RD. P.O. BOX 13819 MILWAUKEE, WI 53213

Visit Hal Leonard Online at
www.halleonard.com

CONTENTS

ANGELS AMONG US

Words and Music by BECKY HOBBS
and DON GOODMAN

(Spoken:) I was walkin' home from school   on a cold winter day.   Took a shortcut through the woods

and I lost my way.   It was get-tin' late ___

BLESS THE BROKEN ROAD

Words and Music by MARCUS HUMMON,
BOBBY BOYD and JEFF HANNA

D.S. al Coda

ANYWAY

Words and Music by BRAD WARREN,
BRETT WARREN and MARTINA McBRIDE

Moderate Ballad

You can spend your whole _ life build - ing some - thing from noth - ing. One storm can come _ and blow _ it all _ a - way. _ Build it an - y - way. _

You can chase _ a dream _ that seems so out of reach, _ and you

sing, _____ I dream, _____ I love _____

an - y - way. _____

BELIEVE

Words and Music by RONNIE DUNN
and CRAIG WISEMAN

Moderately slow

1. Old man Wrig-ley lived _ in that white house
2.-4. *(See additional lyrics)*

down the street where I grew up. Ma-ma used to send

me o-ver with things. _ We struck a friend - ship up. _

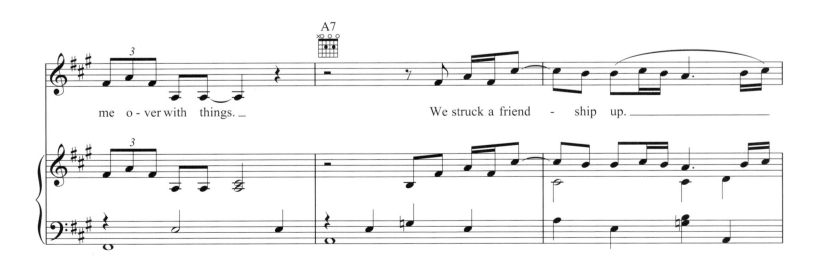

Additional Lyrics

2. Said he was in the war, went in the Navy,
   Lost his wife, lost his baby.
   Broke down and asked him one time:
   "How you keep from goin' crazy?"
   He said, "I'll see my wife and son in just a little while."
   I asked him what he meant, he looked at me and smiled,
   Refrain

3. A few years later I was off at college,
   Talking to Mom on the phone one night.
   Gettin' all caught up on the gossip,
   The ins and outs of the small town life.
   She said, "Oh, by the way, son,
   Old Man Wrigley's died."

4. Later on that night,
   I laid there thinkin' back.
   'Thought about a couple long lost summers,
   I didn't know whether to cry or laugh.
   If there was ever anybody
   'Deserved a ticket to the other side,
   It'd be that sweet old man [who]
   Looked me in the eye,
   Refrain

BLESSED

Words and Music by BRETT JAMES,
HILLARY LINDSEY and TROY VERGES

GO REST HIGH ON THAT MOUNTAIN

Words and Music by
VINCENT GILL

Slowly, in Gospel style

1. I know your
life __ on __ earth was trou - bled __ and on - ly you _____ could know __ the

2. *(See additional lyrics)*

Additional Lyrics

2. Oh, how we cried the day you left us,
   We gathered 'round your grave to grieve.
   I wish I could see the angels' faces
   When they hear your sweet voice sing.
   Chorus

ME AND GOD

Words and Music by
JOSH TURNER

There ain't noth-in' that can't ___ be done by me and God. ___

GOD GAVE ME YOU

Words and Music by
DAVE BARNES

52

gave __ me you. _____

HE AIN'T THE LEAVIN' KIND

Words and Music by MICHAEL DULANEY
and NEIL THRASHER

kind. _____

HELLO WORLD

Words and Music by TOM DOUGLAS,
TONY LANE and DAVID LEE

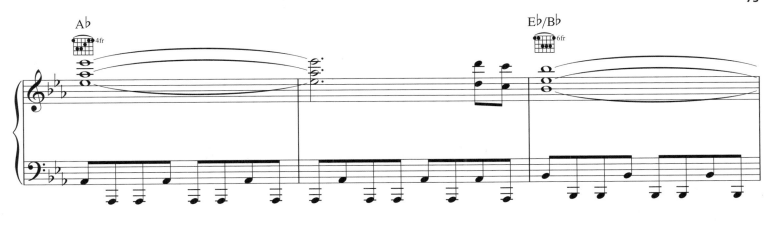

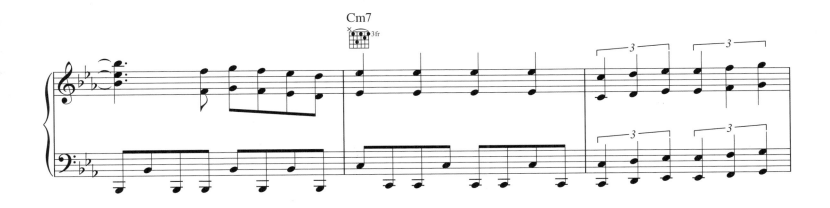

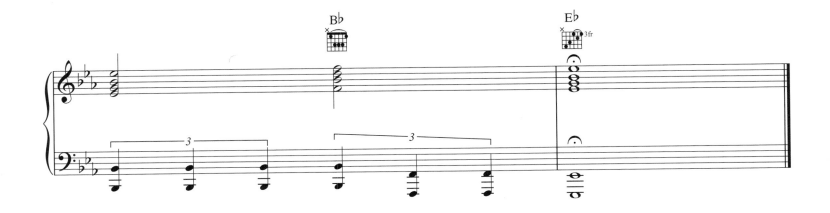

I HOPE YOU DANCE

Words and Music by TIA SILLERS
and MARK D. SANDERS

hope you nev - er lose _____ your sense of the won - der.
nev - er fear ___ those ___ moun - tains in the dis - tance.

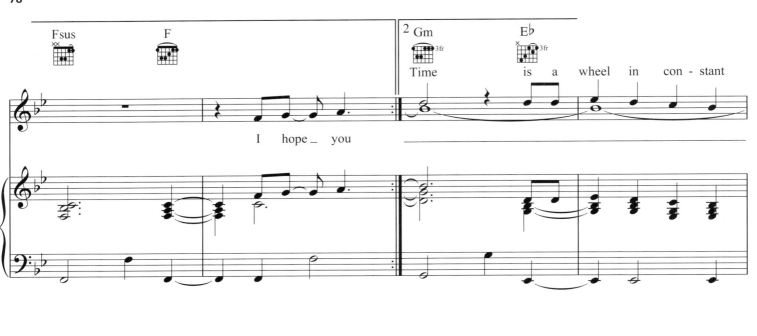

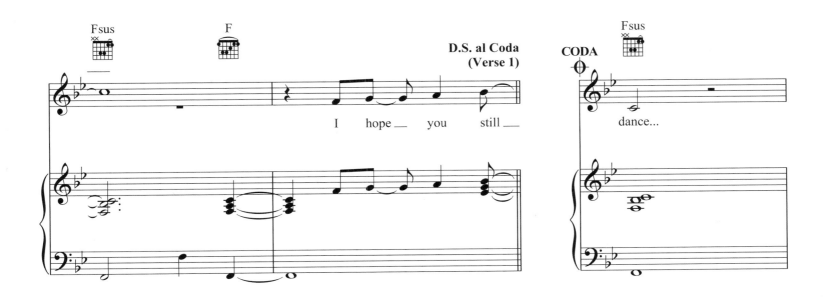

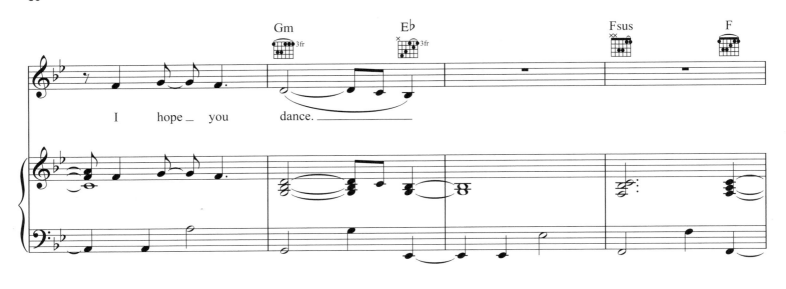

I hope _ you dance. _____

(Time is a wheel in con - stant mo - tion, al -

I hope _ you dance. _____

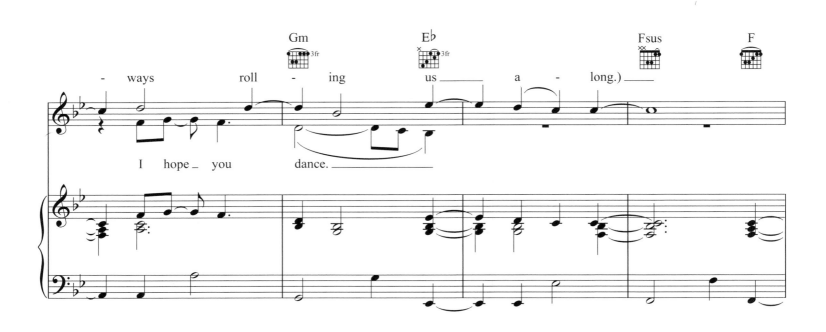

- ways roll - ing us _____ a - long.) _____

I hope _ you dance. _____

(Tell me, who wants to look back on their youth and won-

I hope _ you dance, _____

Repeat and Fade

-der where ___ those years ___ have ___ gone?)

I hope _ you dance. _____

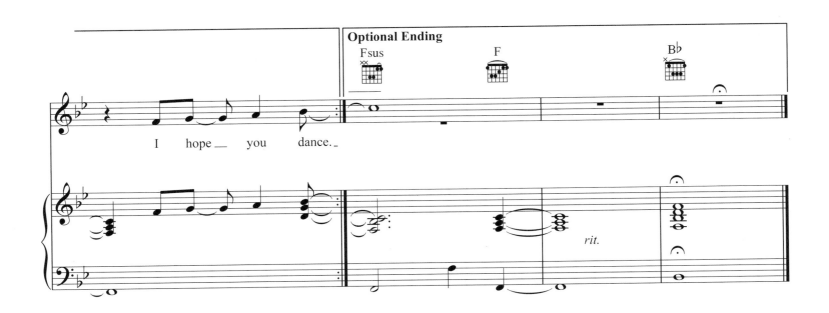

Optional Ending

I hope ___ you dance. _

rit.

IF HEAVEN WASN'T SO FAR AWAY

Words and Music by ROBERT HATCH,
BRETT JONES and DALLAS DAVIDSON

Recorded a half step lower.

JESUS TAKE THE WHEEL

Words and Music by BRETT JAMES,
HILLARY LINDSEY and GORDIE SAMPSON

LONG BLACK TRAIN

Words and Music by
JOSH TURNER

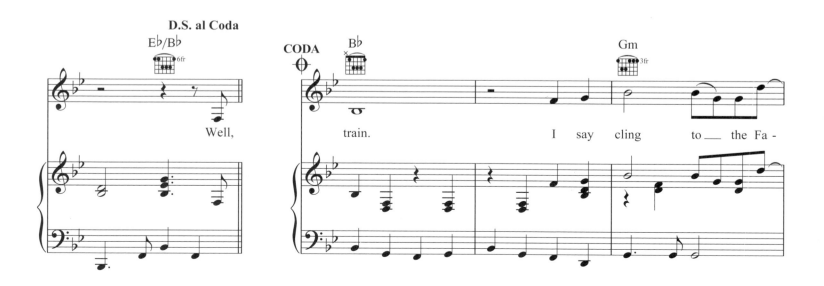

THE MAN I WANT TO BE

Words and Music by BRETT JAMES
and TIM NICHOLS

SAVIOR'S SHADOW

Words and Music by BLAKE SHELTON,
JESSI ALEXANDER and JON RANDALL

I'm stand-ing _ in _ my _ Sav-ior's _ shad - ow.
stand-ing _ in _ my _ Sav-ior's _ shad - ow,
stand-ing _ in _ my _ Sav-ior's _ shad - ow,

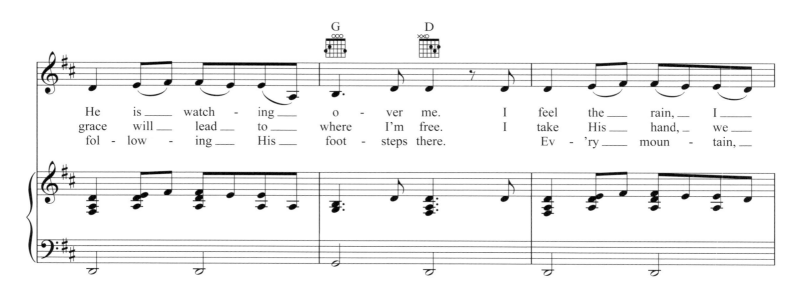

He is _ watch-ing _ o - ver me.   I feel the _ rain, _ I _
grace will _ lead _ to _ where I'm free.   I take His _ hand, _ we _
fol-low-ing _ His _ foot-steps there.   Ev-'ry _ moun-tain, _

won't for-sake me. When I'm ___ in ___ my ___ Sav-ior's ___ shad - ow, I'm

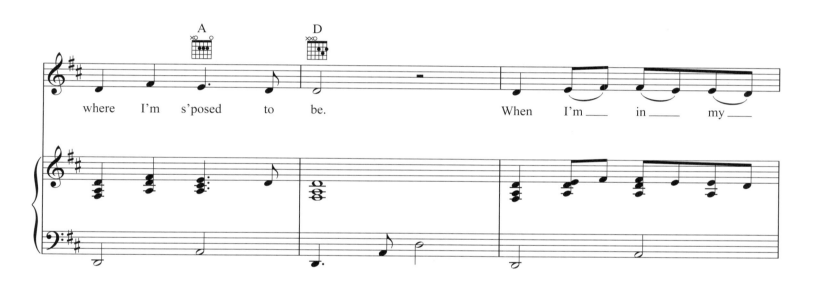

where I'm s'posed to be. When I'm ___ in ___ my ___

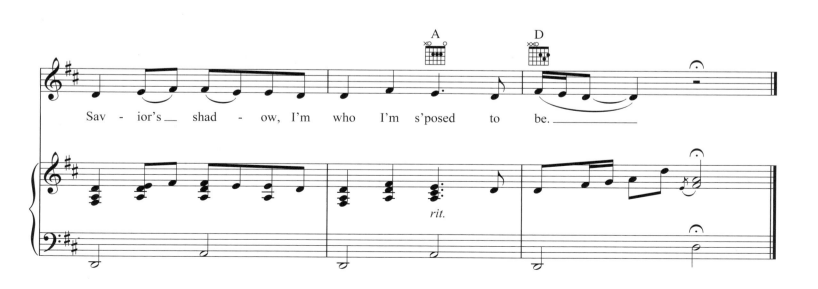

Sav-ior's ___ shad - ow, I'm who I'm s'posed to be. ___

rit.

SOMETHING IN THE WATER

Words and Music by CHRIS DESTEFANO,
CARRIE UNDERWOOD and BRETT JAMES

G

ing a - long __ to "A - maz - ing Grace." __ Can't no - bod - y wipe __ this

Bm

Em7

smile off my face. Got joy _____ in my heart, __ an - gels on my side. __ Thank _

C

___ God al - might __ - y, I _____ saw the light. ___ Gon - na look __

G

___ a - head, __ no turn - ing back, _ live ___ ev - 'ry day __ giv - ing all __

Bm

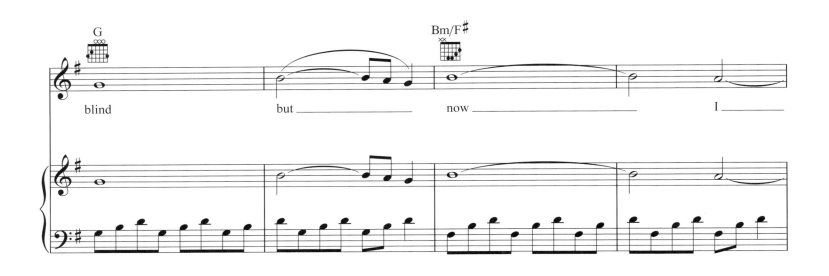

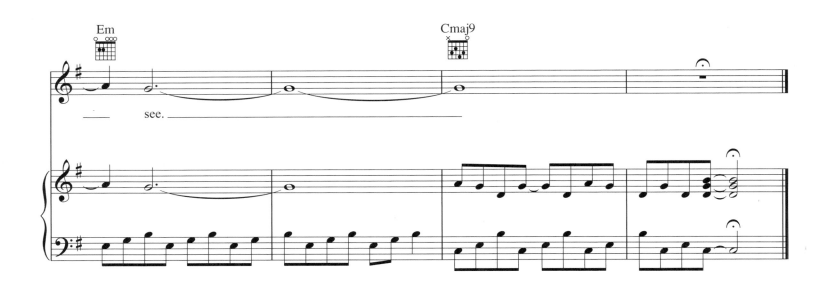

THAT'S WHY I PRAY

Words and Music by DANELLE LEVERETT REEVES,
BLAIR DALY and SARAH BUXTON

Man on the T - V's gone in - sane; ev' - ry - bod - y's just ___ laugh- -ing.

Peo - ple 'cross the world ___ hold - ing on; ___ the earth caved in, the o - cean came ___ down ___ crash - ing. ___

THAT'S WHAT I LOVE ABOUT SUNDAY

Words and Music by ADAM DORSEY
and MARK NARMORE

THREE WOODEN CROSSES

Words and Music by KIM WILLIAMS
and DOUG JOHNSON

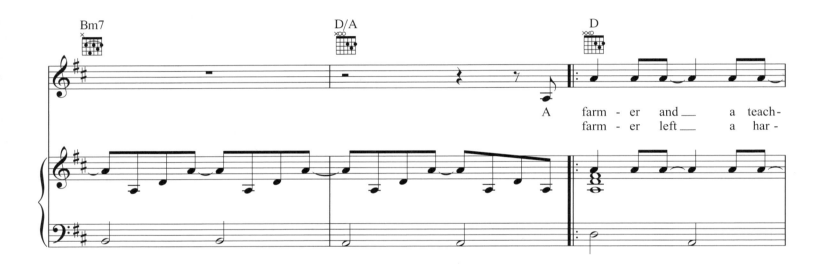

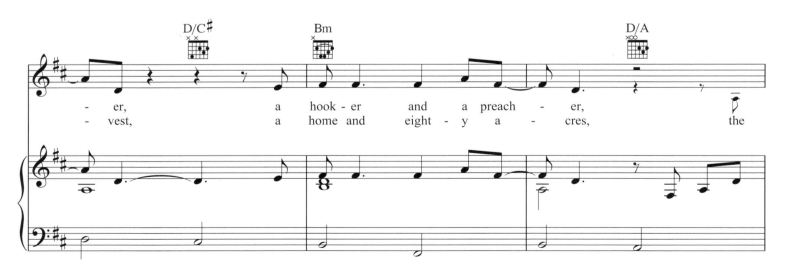

Recorded a half step lower.

WHERE WERE YOU
(When the World Stopped Turning)

Words and Music by
ALAN JACKSON

Where were you when the world ___ stopped turn-in' that Sep - tem - ber

day?

Out in the yard ___ with your wife and chil - dren or

Teach - in' a class ___ full of in - no - cent chil - dren or

WHEN I GET WHERE I'M GOIN'

Words and Music by RIVERS RUTHERFORD
and GEORGE TEREN

HAL LEONARD COUNTRY DECADE SERIES

THE 1950s

50 country golden oldies, including: Ballad of a Teenage Queen • Cold, Cold Heart • El Paso • Heartaches by the Number • Heartbreak Hotel • Hey, Good Lookin' • I Walk the Line • In the Jailhouse Now • Jambalaya (On the Bayou) • Sixteen Tons • Tennessee Waltz • Walkin' After Midnight • Your Cheatin' Heart • and more.
00311283 Piano/Vocal/Guitar $15.99

THE 1970s

41 songs, including: All the Gold in California • Coal Miner's Daughter • Country Bumpkin • The Devil Went to Georgia • The Gambler • Another Somebody Done Somebody Wrong Song • If We Make It Through December • Lucille • Sleeping Single in a Double Bed • and more.
00311285 Piano/Vocal/Guitar $15.99

THE 1980s

40 country standards, including: All My Ex's Live in Texas • The Chair • Could I Have This Dance • Coward of the County • Drivin' My Life Away • Elvira • Forever and Ever, Amen • God Bless the U.S.A. • He Stopped Loving Her Today • I Was Country When Country Wasn't Cool • Islands in the Stream • On the Road Again • Tennessee Flat Top Box • To All the Girls I've Loved Before • What's Forever For • You're the Reason God Made Oklahoma • and more.
00311282 Piano/Vocal/Guitar $15.99

THE 1990s

40 songs, including: Achy Breaky Heart (Don't Tell My Heart) • Amazed • Blue • Boot Scootin' Boogie • Down at the Twist and Shout • Friends in Low Places • The Greatest Man I Never Knew • He Didn't Have to Be • Here's a Quarter (Call Someone Who Cares) • Man! I Feel like a Woman! • She Is His Only Need • Wide Open Spaces • You Had Me from Hello • You're Still the One • and more.
00311280 Piano/Vocal/Guitar $16.95

THE 2000s - 2nd Edition

35 contemporary country classics, including: Alcohol • American Soldier • Beer for My Horses • Blessed • Breathe • Have You Forgotten? • I Am a Man of Constant Sorrow • I Hope You Dance • I'm Gonna Miss Her (The Fishin' Song) • Long Black Train • No Shoes No Shirt (No Problems) • Redneck Woman • Where the Stars and Stripes and the Eagle Fly • Where Were You (When the World Stopped Turning) • and more.
00311281 Piano/Vocal/Guitar $16.99

FOR MORE INFORMATION,
SEE YOUR LOCAL MUSIC DEALER,
OR WRITE TO:

HAL•LEONARD®
CORPORATION
7777 W. BLUEMOUND RD. P.O. BOX 13819
MILWAUKEE, WISCONSIN 53213

Visit Hal Leonard online at
www.halleonard.com

Prices, contents and availability subject to change without notice.

0111